Stop Boring, Start Exciting
Your Customers, Your Employees, and Yourself!

EXCEPTIONALIZE IT!™

LIOR ARUSSY

Published by **4i**
Strativity Group Inc.
Continental Plaza, 401 Hackensack Avenue, Eight Floor
Hackensack, NJ 07601-6411
Tel (201) 843-1315

ISBN 978-0-9826648-2-7

PRINTED IN THE UNITED STATES OF AMERICA

WWW.STRATIVITY.COM

*Dedicated to the exceptional people
I've had the privilege of working with.
Thank you for the Inspiration.*

CONTENTS

CUSTOMER

YOU

MANAGER

SUCCESS

Exceptionalize It! What Is It?

Is it a book? Well, it might be packaged as one. In actuality, it's a manifesto, a call to action, a personal training session, and a mirror, all blended together.

Exceptionalize It! is a reality check for all of us. We live in a world of exceptional or nothing. Just "OK" will no longer satisfy our customers and managers; nor should it satisfy us. We need to accept the reality that if we don't rise up to exceptional performance, we'll write our own ticket to irrelevance. Without exceptionalism in everything we do, we will no longer be relevant as businesses and employees. And when we dig deep down into our dreams and ambitions, we will find that without exceptionalism, we will become a disappointment to ourselves.

Exceptionalize It! is also a manifesto of how to rise to the exceptional performance within us as individuals and our organizations. It is a wakeup call to stop accepting mediocrity and average performance; to stop simply *knowing* what we should do and instead start *doing* those things.

And, yes, these pages will be the mirror that may tell an inconvenient truth. While respecting your achievements to date, staying relevant requires you to constantly examine the simple question: **Are You Exceptional?**

Why Exceptionalize It?

Why is exceptionalism so important now?

The answer is quite simple. You have no other choice.

Both organizations and individuals have new challenges to overcome. Organizations today are facing greater competitive forces and increasingly demanding customers who are using their virtual pens to harshly penalize even the slightest infraction.

Individuals seeking a fulfilling career and life are facing similar forces. Take a look at any reality show and you'll get a sense of the number of people who are chasing the same dream. Examine the activities on the web and you'll discover the millions who are striving for success or fame. In this economy, just take a look at the number of applicants for any desirable open position.

Considering the pressures both companies and individuals are facing, being exceptional is more necessary than ever if you are to stand out. But the rules are constantly changing. The standards are constantly being raised. Meeting expectations is no longer sufficient. Doing your job is not a reason to keep you as an employee. Our customers expect exceptional experiences. Our managers demand exceptional performance. And ultimately, your commitment to excellence requires it.

It's time to accept the truth we are facing and embrace it.

How long will it take you to start to Exceptionalize It?

This book will explore how to *Exceptionalize It!*
across four dimensions:

CUSTOMER　　　YOU　　　MANAGER　　　SUCCESS

Together these elements paint a complete picture of what
to "exceptionalize" and how to *Exceptionalize It!* in all the
different parts of our business life. Welcome to the journey.

CUSTOMER

The Customer's Choice

Your organization's success is dependent on your customers.
Without them, you're out of business. More accurately,
your organization depends on a customer's choice to:

> purchase from you
>
> buy at your asking price
>
> use your products properly
>
> forgive your mistakes
>
> service the products exclusively with you
>
> come back and purchase more
>
> not badmouth you
>
> recommend you

Yes, you are subject to the customer's choice. (Some, such as
public service, health care, and other organizations have been
slow to recognize this fact, but it will hit them eventually.)
The essence of your business is influencing customer choices.
You do so by innovating products and services and designing
and delivering exceptional experiences. But the goal is clear:
becoming the customer choice.

The foundation to *Exceptionalize It!* for companies is the
recognition that we are submitting ourselves to the customer's
choice. We are in the customer choice business. The customer
makes choices. We need to impact them. The ultimate choice
is with the customer.

EXCEPTIONALIZE IT!™

How will you influence customers to choose you?

Meeting Expectations Is Boring

So how can we impact customer choices? Every action we take influences current and prospective customers' choices. Deliver a "me too" product and the customer will choose the competition. Surprise the customer with a memorable experience, and you might just create a customer for life (and a profitable one at that).

The journey starts with your goals. Most organizations are structured simply to meet customer expectations. *Boring!* And when customers are bored, they seek excitement. If you don't provide it, your competitors will.

Boredom is a key reason that many personal relationships end. The partners seek excitement and rejuvenation. Predictability eventually fails to fulfill the human needs.

Because we work with humans, the same is true in the commercial world. Many organizations are set up to simply meet customer expectations and then are surprised that loyalty doesn't follow. It's difficult to be loyal to boredom. It is against customers' nature.

The first step on the journey to *Exceptionalize It!* is to accept the fact that customer experience goals are set too low. It's time to recognize customers' needs for the unique, interesting, and stimulating. It's time to stop boring customers and raise our goals to pleasantly surprise them.

EXCEPTIONALIZE IT!™

Stop boring your customers.

Select Your Customers

Yes, you read it right. Not every customer is king. The *right* customer is king. This is a practice I established in all the businesses I've been a part of. I refused to do business with every customer who knew how to spell my name and had a budget. Some of them are abusive. Some have unrealistic expectations. Some of them are not willing to pay a price that respects the value I deliver. So I stopped chasing every customer and started to spend more time qualifying the right customers.

When I got stuck with the wrong customer, I fired them. Your business needs to be profitable. Doing business with the wrong customers will produce the opposite results. You want a win-win situation? Send your wrong customers to your competitors. And now you've won twice. You've freed up time to delight the right customers and gotten your competitors stuck with losses due to unprofitable customers.

A certain type of customer will appreciate your true value. Not all will understand it, appreciate, or be willing to pay for it. Focus on the right customers and treat them like kings. Create an exceptional experience specifically for them based on their needs and interests. You will then, and only then, establish a profitable and enjoyable business.

EXCEPTIONALIZE IT!™

Stop chasing every customer. Focus on the RIGHT customers.

Your Universal Competitors

Do you know your competitors? Sure you do. You have competitive analyses somewhere in your organization detailing each of your primary competitors. Well, all organizations around the world face two universal competitors. But those competitors are often either overlooked or misunderstood.

"Doing nothing" is your first universal competitor. The customer choice not to act on your offer is a form of competition that prevents you from establishing a relationship. Simply put, the customer chooses not to act. Why? They are not impressed. The customer does not see a burning reason to choose you. Being without you seems more desirable to the customer.

"Good enough" is your other universal competitor. A customer's choice to stay with the existing chosen solution basically states, "I do not see any exceptionalism." Good enough is a form of rejection that results from your failure to demonstrate exceptional differences between you and customer's current choice.

Pay attention to these universal competitors. They will tell you more about the state of your exceptionalism than a desperate competitor that is too eager to offer discounts.

☺

EXCEPTIONALIZE IT!™

Drive your customers to choose you.

Welcome to the Best-in-the-World Competition

"How did customers become so picky?" you wonder. You know your industry. All the players are kind of average. Where did the customer develop these high expectations? Welcome to competing against the best in the world.

It is a mistake for you to believe that, because the rest of your industry is not customer focused, you can get away with similar performance. Customers shop all over. They stay at best-in-the-world hotels. They patronize best-in-the-world restaurants. They enjoy best-in-the-world entertainment. In short, your customers are no longer comparing you to the best in your industry. They compare you to the best of their experiences. You no longer reside in your product-centric industry. You compete against of the best-in-the-world brands that surround your customers. And compared to them, you are… well, you get the point.

To set the goals of *Exceptionalize It!* correctly, you need to understand the new world of competitors you're facing. You're not in Kansas anymore. You are in the customer world. In this world, emotions and aspirations are being fulfilled in different ways. And the best-in-the-world brands win.

☺

EXCEPTIONALIZE IT!™

Are you ready to play
on the customer's
best-in-the-world stage?

Customer Advantage or Competitive Advantage

It's so much fun to beat the competition, isn't it? The laser focus on the next competitive move blinds organizations. The search for competitive advantage sometimes comes at the expense of listening to customer needs and creating the right experience for the customers.

I used to work in the technology world and we were obsessed with catching up with competitors' features. We just forgot to ask the customers if they cared about any of them. And most of the time they didn't. We were glorifying our own technological prowess and making our products more complex and confusing. Customers wanted simplification.

Stop chasing your competitors. They don't pay your bills. Focus on creating customer advantage. Capture the needs and aspirations of your customers, and then innovate your experience based on that knowledge. Instead of focusing on winning industry awards, it is time to focus on winning customers' hearts (and wallets).

Top organizations define their own path through customer innovation. Exceptionalizing it, for these organizations, is all about delighting the customers. The competition is merely background noise. The ultimate prize and recognition is the customer's choice.

EXCEPTIONALIZE IT!™

Innovate for customers, not to outdo the competition.

☺
—

Who Is Spoiling Your Customers?

A common mistake among corporations is to compare themselves to their industry competitors. They all read the same industry trade magazines and websites and follow the same industry experts' advice. In the meantime, vendors outside of your industry are delighting your customers. This reshapes their customer expectations and standards. Your customers may enjoy an amazing vacation on Royal Caribbean Cruise Lines or a wonderful first-class flight on Singapore Airlines. They may enjoy a Cirque du Soleil show or get pampered at a Ritz Carlton spa. These amazing experiences will be transformed into lasting memories that will then guide their selection of vendors and products in other industries.

Following amazing experiences delivered by world-class companies, customers will impose their new standards on you. They will demand the same level of delight and excitement. They will accept nothing but the exceptional. And if you fail to provide it, as many of your industry competitors will, you will be subject to price pressure.

The real question you need to answer is not what your industry competitors do differently, but rather who is delighting and spoiling your customers? The answer to this question is most often outside of your industry.

Who is evolving the standards? What are your customers' new expectations based on those experiences? Understand who is pampering and delighting your customers and you will define your new agenda for customer delight.

EXCEPTIONALIZE IT!™

Your future is being shaped by vendors outside of your industry. Discover who is spoiling your customers.

☺

Create a Natural Attraction

There is one major difference between companies that *Exceptionalize It!* and those that don't (even though they think they do). When you *Exceptionalize It!* customers stand in line for your products and services. You don't need to chase customers, they chase you. You don't need to discount heavily or increase your sales and marketing costs; customers come to you. Why? Because you deliver exceptional value worth the price you charge.

And, because the number of companies that *Exceptionalize It! is* limited, they enjoy greater popularity. Their competitors, in the meantime, think that boring performance is acceptable and fall into a wishful-thinking trap.

Proving that you are truly exceptionalizing it is simple: How difficult is it for you to attract new customers? How costly is it for you to retain customers? What price do you pay to build customer loyalty? If the answers to these questions are, "Too difficult," "Too costly," and "Too much," then you are not exceptionalizing it yet. You are merely delivering boring performance, which creates yawning responses among your customers.

When you *Exceptionalize It!* you create a natural attraction. Your customers gravitate toward your products and away from your competitors and the payoff is every company's dream: profitable growth. The economics of your customer relationship will show you very clearly why exceptionalizing it is the most profitable way to do business.

EXCEPTIONALIZE IT!™

What do you need to
do to naturally
attract customers
to you?

Are Customers Cheaters?

Here is an honest question to consider: Do you believe that all your customers are cheaters unless proven otherwise? Or do you believe they are all trustworthy unless proven otherwise? You're probably now protesting with the classic, "It depends. Some are and some aren't." Well, my question is not just a philosophical question. It goes back to how you treat all of your customers. Do you design processes, products, and services generously because you believe that the majority of your customers are honest and fair when conducting business with you?

Often, when I work with clients and examine their processes and the way they address customers, I'll comment that they act as if all customers are cheaters. And that is when the story comes: "Well, in 1978 we had that customer who tricked us…and that is why we needed to change the process." In the meantime they have punished tens of thousands, if not millions, of customers throughout the years who were all honest and fair. One bad customer makes business leaders suspicious and guarded.

All too often, we miss the opportunity to deliver exceptional performance because we don't trust our customers. We approach them in a guarded and suspicious way because of bad experiences we had with just a few customers in the past. But, above all, we penalize ourselves. We miss the chance to delight our customers by fully delivering our best very quickly, the belief that all customers are cheaters creeps into our minds, processes, and products. This turns the relationship into a competitive one where there is one winner and one loser. We do not want to be the loser. Instead, we need to trust our customers, and in doing so, allow ourselves to deliver an exceptional experience to them. In return, we'll gain their trust—and more of their business.

EXCEPTIONALIZE IT!™

Trust your customers.
Stop punishing all
customers for the few
problematic customers.

☺

The Relationship Account Rules

Relationships with customers, like relationships in life, are built on a give-and-take system. Imagine a relationship bank account with your customers. The bank account rules are very simple:

Rule Number 1
You cannot make a withdrawal without making a deposit.

Rule Number 2
The size of your withdrawals is limited
to the size of your deposits.

As such, if you want your customers to be loyal and purchase exclusively from you (huge withdrawal), be ready to make a similar commitment (huge deposits). It's that simple. If your customers resist being loyal to you or paying your asking price, it means that your mutual relationship bank account does not have sufficient funds (a.k.a. memories and value). The rejections you face are based on your lack of investment. You didn't create an exceptional experience for the customer that merits his reciprocation with a similar exceptional commitment to you. When the customer asks for a discount, she is merely saying "insufficient funds"—the same message you will hear from your banker when you attempt to withdraw more than you have deposited.

Keep your relationship bank account fully stocked with exceptional experiences and lasting memories, and your customers will reward you with the loyalty and profitability you seek.

☺

EXCEPTIONALIZE IT!™

How much did
you deposit in your
customer relationship
bank account today?

Be Authentic

Anyone who's ever visited Orlando, Florida, is familiar with the phenomen. There is one Disney World and dozens of amusement parks that try to copy it. They also have mascots and rides, but none are Disney. That is why Disney commands customer loyalty and premium prices while the others discount their tickets to draw in customers. Additionally, Disney sells memorabilia in quantities that far outpace the memorabilia sales of the other parks.

In life and in business there is the original and there are the copycats. What is your value proposition? Are you original? Do you have an authentic value to offer to your customers? Are you unique and differentiated? To maintain a long-term relationship with your customers, you need to find your core of originality. Customers are attracted to authentic value and people. They belittle copycats.

Design and deliver original experiences for your customers and they will repay you with genuine commitment. Deliver a "me too" solution and you will find yourself frustrated and chasing customers with ridiculous offers. So stop being someone else and find your original core that will attract customers naturally to you.

☺

EXCEPTIONALIZE IT!™

Be original and deliver authentic experiences.

Clear, Colorful, Credible Future

Customers don't buy products. They buy a beautiful future. Success belongs to those who manage to paint a clear, colorful future for their customers and then integrate their products and services into it. Customers want to know that their investment will last and will fit their lifestyle.

When creating experiences for customers, develop a clear future the customer can relate to. Make it colorful and vibrant so the customer wants to be part of it and, most importantly make it credible. The fact that the future you describe is appealing doesn't mean you can deliver it. Make sure that you have a credible role in delivering that future. Describe your ability to deliver on the promise based on your track record, otherwise customers may assume that it will be yet another unfulfilled promise resulting in disappointment and resentment.

EXCEPTIONALIZE IT!™

Stop selling products; start developing your customer's future.

☺

Engage Using Aspirations, Not Functionality

As salespeople, we're programmed to look for the tangibles. We sell a tangible product or service, so we strive to understand the tangible needs of the customer. Then, when we try to close the deal, we spell out the product functionality. This is when we lose the customer.

A product's functionality is merely a component of the overall needed solution. When a customer buys a candle, it's not just a form of lighting she's buying. It may be part of an occasion, like a birthday celebration or a funeral; it may be purchased as home decor or as a gift. Failing to understand the human aspect of the customer need is failing to understand the full story.

Always strive to sell to the human aspirations and recognize that the technical requirements are merely a vehicle to achieve those aspirations. From his perspective, the customer pays to achieve his aspirations, not gain the product functionality.

☺

EXCEPTIONALIZE IT!™

Discover the human story behind the customer's functional requirements.

☺

The Experience Building Blocks

So how do you build exceptional experiences? There are five simple building blocks to create customer delight and amazement. These are the 5 Es of Exceptional Experiences.

Easy –Make it easy to do business with you. Always focus on reducing wasted time when interacting with you. Demonstrate respect for his or her time and efforts.

Educate –Teach your customer something new. Every interaction should leave the customer with new, meaningful insight. The customer should feel that you are empowering him or her with useful knowledge.

Engage – Conduct an authentic dialogue with your customers, and encourage each customer to engage with likeminded customers. Be the connector that enhances the customer's network and helps him to be more successful.

Explore – Allow your customers to explore new and exciting areas by enabling them to build her own creations using your products and services. Don't just provide a one-size-fits-all solution. Allow your customer to express herself through your products. (If you don't, your competitors will.)

Exceptional –Recognize individuality and communicate with him in ways that are relevant to him. In moments of truth, when the customer needs you the most, shine. Deliver exceptional performance that demonstrates that your relationship is here to stay.

There are a multitude of opportunities to delight customers and strengthen customer relationships with exceptional performance. The more you *Exceptionalize It!* the fuller your customer relationship bank account will be. (And the bigger the future withdrawals will be, of course).

EXCEPTIONALIZE IT!™

How many of the five Es are you using today?

Don't Fall into the Discount Trap

"I want a discount." Sound familiar? If your organization is like most businesses, your salespeople will try to dance around the request but eventually will succumb to it.

Allow me to provide a new perspective on this age-old issue. When a customer asks for a discount, here's what he's really saying: "I see your product and I see your price. I just can't see the link between them." Now you face two choices:

1. Provide the discount—and reaffirm to the customer that your product is in fact inferior and is not worth the price you asked for.

2. Deliver and demonstrate value that justifies your price.

In short, a request for a discount is an indication that the customer is bored. It is a sign the customer considers you no different than the competition. So, he's opting for the only factor left to differentiate: the price.

The choice is yours. Either deliver on the discount request (but this *is not* a way to *Exceptionalize It!*) or deliver exceptional value and an exceptional experience that your customer will not dispute is worth your asking price.

EXCEPTIONALIZE IT!™

End discounting, start
exceptionalizing.

Stop Selling

No one likes to be sold to. No one likes salespeople. Customers don't buy things against their will. (Sorry to disappoint all the "rainmaker" salespeople.) Customers like to discover. They like to explore and engage with new experiences.

As a person engaging with your customers, your role is to inspire, excite, amaze, educate, and ultimately invite the customer to join your products, services, and experiences story. If you educate and inspire customers, they will buy naturally and pay full price. If you fail to amaze, you will need to resort to old sales trickery, which rarely works and results in low-margin one-time deals, at best.

Selling is a mind-set that assumes that you can force a customer into a deal they don't really want. It's a behavior that treats customers as if they are walking wallets. It must stop. It is disrespectful and ineffective in dealing with today's empowered customers. Customers will only buy on their own terms. Your role is to inspire, educate, excite, and amaze so they will want to be part of your story. Be the Chief Inspirer.

EXCEPTIONALIZE IT!™

Stop selling, start inspiring your customers.

☺

An Authentic Smile Is Priceless

Throughout the years, when I presented these ideas at workshops and conferences, I got the occasional comment, "We don't have the margins to do all this" or "We don't have the time to deliver exceptional experiences." My response is quite simple: "How much does it cost you to smile?"

The customer experience consists of attributes and attitudes. You may not have the funds to invest in attribute improvements, but attitudes are free. An authentic smile, a caring statement, a personal note—these do not cost money or take much time. They're a matter of mind-set. If you love your customers, you will do it naturally. If you think they're your enemy, you won't.

Start with a positive attitude, which includes making sure you see your customers not as foes, but rather as friends. Add small acts of kindness that will strengthen customer relationships and build loyalty. Business will follow, and then you'll have the margins to invest in the attributes of the experience and raise them to an exceptional level.

Start your exceptional performance with an exceptional smile. It is not expensive, but it is priceless.

EXCEPTIONALIZE IT!™

Did you brighten your customers' day today?

☺

Generosity: The Best Investment

Generosity is the best investment someone can make in a relationship, personal or professional. When you're generous you indicate to your customer that you care about them and are here for the long run. Generosity demonstrates to the customer that you're not just trying to maximize profits in the short term, but rather are committed to the longevity of the relationship.

Generosity comes in different forms. One way is to provide a free lesson or other complimentary service to your customer; another is to help them optimize the usage of the product they purchased from you. Such an act of generosity will ensure your customer's satisfaction and enjoyment.

As pressure increases to maximize short-term gains, we get tunnel vision, focusing solely on meeting our revenue and profits target—now. Relax. Calm down. This urgency to make the numbers is sending the wrong message to your customers. And they will often take advantage of it. Take a deep breath and invest in the long term. You will always have numbers to meet next quarter, and then next year, and then the following year. Don't maximize your short-term revenues at the expense of the future. Build your future success by being generous today.

EXCEPTIONALIZE IT!™

How did you demonstrate generosity and invest in your future?

The Margins Are in the Memories

If you've been to a Disney theme park, you know that the experience is amazing. At the end of almost every attraction there is a gift shop stocked with Disney products priced at high margins. Why is it that people are willing to pay top dollar for Disney-themed clothes and toys?

The answer: The margins are in the stories and memories, not in the technical aspects of the product. If you want to improve your margins, you need to improve your memories first.

EXCEPTIONALIZE IT!™

How powerful are the
memories you create for
your customers?

☺

Show Me the Value

It happens every time: You shower your customer with freebies and somehow he doesn't seem to appreciate it. Free training, free extras, free consulting, free software, you name it; some companies give away the store to attract customers' attention. You're making multiple generous gestures to demonstrate your commitment to the relationship. The problem starts with the concept of a freebie. If it's free, it probably is not worth much, the customer thinks. Although freebies are generous—thus a positive way to show your commitment to the relationship—by positioning them as freebies you undermine them. You need to show their worth.

Let's get to the heart of the issue. Why doesn't your customer appreciate all that you're doing for him? Because he doesn't know the value, in dollars, of the extra services you provide. You assume that the customer knows the value. How would he if you don't tell him? He never needed to purchase those services because they came for free. Demonstrate the value associated with your exceptional performance.

Here is a quick-win practice you can and should start immediately. Every time you offer a customer a generous service, price it. Provide the customer with that price and even an invoice, and then you can waive the price. By doing so, you create further deposits in the customer relationship bank account. Creating value visualization tools will enable your customers to understand the investment you make in them and the exceptional value you deliver to them.

☺

EXCEPTIONALIZE IT!™

How will you show customers the financial value of the exceptional performance you provide?

Stop Promising, Start Delivering

When you review a company's overall budget, an interesting disparity becomes clear. The budgets for sales and marketing are disproportionately greater than the budget for customer service. Sales and marketing is when a company makes promises to customers. Customer service is when it delivers. Companies seem to be more proficient in painting beautiful pictures of the future than actually delivering them.

It is time to correct this disparity. Companies that win in the race for the customer invest in delivering the future, not just in promising it. Find out what areas in your "delivery" system are weak or dysfunctional and fix them, whether it's customer service processes or product functionality, shipping issues or billing errors. The most credible statement you can make is not the one made by a salesperson, but rather one made by delivering on what you promise. When the sales pitch is exceptional, the customers' expectations are heightened to levels that are almost impossible to satisfy. When service is exceptional, you create a loyal customer. Invest heavily in delivering, not in promising.

EXCEPTIONALIZE IT!™

It's time to be exceptional in delivering to customers, not in promising the exceptional.

☺

Shine in Service Recovery

Let's face it. Mistakes are going to happen. Despite all your process redesign, you're working with people who are human, not automatons, therefore not always adhere to your processes. This may lead to poor performance that will disappoint your customers. Then what?

A simple apology and move on? Not if you try to *Exceptionalize It!* Research shows that companies that *wowed* their customers during a difficult time enjoyed an increase in customer loyalty. In fact, customers who were during difficult times demonstrated greater loyalty than *wowed* customers who experienced no problem at all. What's the logic? Exceptional resolution during a difficult situation is a demonstration of commitment. It illustrates to customers that you're here for the long run. It proves to customers that they do business with real people and not with a bureaucracy.

So go ahead and design a program to wow customers during difficult times. Create a plan to demonstrate to customers how much you love them, especially in times when they are in pain. Deliver exceptional performance when your customers need it most. Your customers may expect to lose the argument; instead, show them your generous side and win them over.

☺

EXCEPTIONALIZE IT!™

How will you show your customers love during difficult times?

Accept the Equality in the Relationship

The customer is king. You've heard this so many times it has become a cliché. But do you believe in it? Does your company behave as if the customer is king? Do you allow customers to have a choice in the way their relationship is conducted? Can you say that you treat the customer as an equal? If you're honest with yourself, the answer will be, "Not really."

We treat customers like spoiled children. If they scream, we buy their silence with bribes and gifts. We don't conduct a true dialogue with them. We don't ask their opinion. We decide for them. If you disagree, just check what happened to the last customer surveys your company conducted. How much change was made based on the insight gained from those surveys? How quickly did you take action? Most companies take incremental action, if they take any action at all.

Why is this the case? Because deep down, we still believe we know better than the customer. Deep down, we think we are superior to them. It's ingrained in our corporate culture to treat them not as an equal, but as a source of revenue—the cheapest way to make our numbers. It's only when we change that culture to one that treats customers as equals in a value exchange that we'll have a chance to gain their loyalty.

EXCEPTIONALIZE IT!™

How do you treat your customers?

Customer Championship or Market Leader?

What do you want to be when you grow up? A market leader or a customer champion? Do you want to be the largest company in your market or the one everyone loves? It's only possible to do both if you *Exceptionalize It!*

There are clear tradeoffs between being a market leader and being a customer champion. Market leaders often chase every customer in the pursuit of size and sacrifice profitability in the process. With shrinking margins, they rarely budget the resources necessary to delight customers. Their customers have less reason to be loyal. Customer champions, on the other hand, stay focused on the customer and use their margins to create delightful reasons for customers to remain loyal. Customers have no reason to go elsewhere, because customer champions continually show their commitment.

Few companies succeed at both. Those who succeed in becoming market leaders yet stay true customer champions have made exceptionalizing it for their customers a very clear priority. Thus, being a customer champion absolutely comes first. The market leadership is the side benefit, not the main purpose of a company's existence. These organizations keep a clear set of values in which investment in customers is key and profitability is its measure. If they need to sacrifice profitability to acquire new customers, then they will think twice about whether those customers should be pursued in the first place. They ensure that they do business with customers they can serve well and remain customer champions for.

Don't confuse yourself. Be very clear about your goals. Market leadership or customer championship, what is the purpose of your existence?

EXCEPTIONALIZE IT!™

Be a customer champion.
It's the profitable way to
run a business.

The Formula of WOW and Exceptionalism

WOW = Impressing and surprising our customers. Everything the customer is already expecting is taken for granted and needs to be delivered flawlessly; then and only then, can wow kick in. By definition "wow" (i.e., exceptional performance) is anything that is beyond customer expectations. If you didn't see surprise on your customer's face, you failed to wow. You succeeded in delivering the expected performance, but the memory will fade rather quickly.

To deliver exceptional experiences, the litmus test is: did you surprise the customer? Did your customer compliment you by saying, "I didn't expect that"? Over time the impressed customer will no longer be surprised by your impressive gestures, but rather, will grow to expect them. That's when you'll need to raise your game and deliver the next surprise. The formula for exceptionalism and wow is ongoing improvement and searching for the next opportunity to impress and surprise customers.

EXCEPTIONALIZE IT!™

How did you impress and surprise your customers today?

The Ultimate Proof:
Are They Standing In Line?

In business there are two possible scenarios. Either you chase customers or customers chase you. Selling commodity products, companies need to invest heavily in courting customers and convincing them to choose their products. Delivering amazing experiences will make customers stand in line and be willing to pay a premium for the privilege of doing business with you—even if you sell a commodity.

It is that simple. If you need to chase your customer, your experience is not good enough. Customer satisfaction is nice. But customer actions are what's profitable.

Your competition is not standing still. They're working full throttle to get customers to choose them. Your competitors are trying to delight customers and obtain their commitment. You are not alone in this race.

So how do you know that you have arrived? When the customers are standing in line for your products. When they are willing to wait until you have availability. When they wake up early in the morning and queue for hours to get one of the first new products you've innovated. That's when you know you've exceptionalized it. Until then, you will continue to chase your customers. Chasing customers gets expensive. The better option is to innovate a new way to amaze them. Deliver beyond their wildest expectations and make yourself indispensable.

☺

EXCEPTIONALIZE IT!™

Are you chasing your customers or are they chasing you?

☺

YOU

What Did You Want to Be When You Grew Up?

Ask a group of adults about their childhood dreams and they'll share with you an elaborate tale. Some dreamed of becoming an astronaut, teacher, ballerina, doctor, or athlete. They all wanted to achieve something great. They all wanted to become someone important and help others or make a difference in the world.

Not surprisingly, no one I polled with that question answered, "I wanted to add value to stockholders." Corporate mission statements commonly include a line about adding value to stockholders, yet that is the least of our ambitions as children or adults. But it's the mantra business leaders put in front of employees every day. We measure success through the narrow lenses of stock prices and performance. No wonder most employees check out and get disengaged.

This is not a dream they aspire to. This is not a goal they are willing to *Exceptionalize It!* for. This is not an objective that will make them wake up an hour early or stay an hour later to complete a project.

Adding value to stockholders is and should be a byproduct of an organization's excellent performance. It should not be the focal point if we want employees to engage with customers and exceptionalize their performance to help build customer loyalty. We should focus ourselves, our employees, and our organizations on creating an impact with the performance we deliver to customers, not shareholders. Impact performance will lead to profitability—and later to stockholder value—by emphasizing customer experience. In many organizations that means the narrative must change, and the daily discussions about goals the organization is working to achieve must change.

EXCEPTIONALIZE IT!™

No one aspires to work for stockholders. Change the narrative of your performance.

Who's Best

Following a multiyear study that polled more than 50,000 participants, we discovered that employees and customers are operating on two different platforms. Employees often rank their performance as exceptional, while customers, who are the recipients of that performance rank it much lower. What employees consider to be the best often does not match customers' definition of the best. Therefore, employees deliver "the best" as defined by them or their managers; customers often disagree with that definition.

It is imperative that "the best" customer experience is defined by those who receive it: customers. You should set your sights as high as your customers' definition of "the best." Don't focus your sights on your own internal standards; this leads to a customer experience that's underwhelming instead of exceptional. The result is that customer satisfaction is low and loyalty is absent. As a result, you'll get frustrated and may even consider customers to be ungrateful and unfair.

It's time to fix the root cause. The misalignment stems from the different definitions. To be exceptional, we need to perform to the customer definition of exceptional, not ours. It's time to understand what that definition is and provide the performance, tools, and resources to deliver it.

EXCEPTIONALIZE IT!™

Who's "best" are you
delivering, yours or
your customers'?

Cynicism:
How Does It Work for You?

Many talented people who were disappointed early or often in life developed an attitude of cynicism. As a form of self-preservation they dismiss any notion of exceptionalism. Their minds are trained to be dismissive of every authentic attempt to shine and deliver excellence. They will always find the flaw in every new idea.

To all the cynics out there, here is a question to ponder: How well does cynicism work for you? Are you happier for it? Do you feel your life is meaningful? Are you looking forward to the years to come? If you are honest with yourself, you will discover that the answer to all these questions is a resounding no.

Cynicism is a short-term break with long-term consequences. Don't get addicted to it. It is time to reconnect, re-believe, and recommit. There is no other way. Gather your strength and find hope in your power to make a difference. Use the power you do have to deliver exceptional performance and to help customers.

EXCEPTIONALIZE IT!™

Focus on the power
you do have and
inspire yourself.

Cynicism Is Not Funny

Cynicism might seem funny at first. But when looking at the big picture, it's not funny at all. Cynicism is often used as a sarcastically humorous way to say, "My boss is a moron and my CEO is incompetent." It's the language of frustrated employees who have "checked out" and are no longer delivering their top performance. They're disengaged, often throwing mud at any great idea.

Show me a cynical organization and I will show you subpar performance. No organization that I know of can deliver passion, pride, and commitment to exceptional performance with cynical employees. Cynicism is the cancer that eats up the exceptional performance in your employees and your organization. Cynical employees follow the rules and don't bother to perform beyond that basic level.

You need to uproot the cynicism in your organization. But you can't simply command it out of your employees. If it took root in their soul, a memo will not make it go away. You need to go back to the cause of the problem. What made your employees cynical? Most likely, they weren't cynical when they joined your company. What happened that transformed their performance into cynical behavior?

EXCEPTIONALIZE IT!™

Uproot cynicism to inspire exceptionalism.

What Do You Move?

Product-centric companies are focused on moving products. They make predefined products and then try to sell them to as many customers as possible. Customer-centric companies move people. They create experiences that move their customers emotionally. Who do you move? Do you move products or do you move people?

Remember, products are merely tools. By being product-centric you view your customers as consumers of those tools. Experiences are complete solutions. When you are customer-centric you view customers as human beings. To move people you need to see them as unique individuals. To move people you must understand their emotions. And, ultimately, you need to be willing to provide a complete solution, not just products.

If your performance is product-centric, moving products become routine. You fail to see the human side of the people who buy your products. In contrast, employees who are customer-centric never forget the people they have the privilege to serve. They enjoy and are energized by being part of people's lives. They are, after all, not only moving products but also moving people. Customer-centric employees create stories that become part of their customers' lives. Start creating memorable stories by becoming customer centric.

EXCEPTIONALIZE IT!™

Move people, not products.

No One Made a Statue in Honor of a Committee

I love that saying. There is so much truth to it. When transformation is preached to the organization, everyone agrees with the idea, and then they wait for the committee to go do it. The reality is that committees do not produce excellence and exceptionalism. They often settle for the lowest common denominator agreed upon by executives with conflicting agendas. The outcome of committees' work is bland and undifferentiated. It's not bold or exciting. It's not a way to *Exceptionalize It!*

So you have a choice. Wait for the committee to reduce the greater transformation into a meaningless incremental project, or take charge and do something bold that will be exceptional, surprising, and delightful to customers. Gather your power and begin to transform your organization's customer experience. While the committee is deliberating, you can already affect hundreds of customers and create a reason for them to be loyal.

Throughout the generations, statues were created to honor the individuals who led change—not for those who waited for instructions.

EXCEPTIONALIZE IT!™

Be the force of change.
Don't wait for the
committee.

Are You Part of the Problem or Part of the Solution?

You have a choice: be part of the problem or part of the solution. If spend your time complaining about your company, CEO, strategy, the latest cost-cutting program, fill in the blank, you're part of the problem. If people around you hear negativity from you (even if it is packaged in a pseudo-funny joke at the company's expense), you're part of the problem. If your days are filled with different ways to document and discuss what's wrong with your company, well, you get the point. Inaction is another way to contribute to the problem and to sustain it. By refraining from action, you propagate the problem.

Being part of the solution is doing the exact opposite. It is rejection of all cynical jokes and recognition of their hazardous impact on the organization's future. Being part of the solution is taking initiative and using the power you do have to make a difference. It's about planning for a better future; working with others to combine resources and apply them to a positive outcome. It's not sitting still and accepting the status quo; it's taking charge and taking action. It might be difficult while surrounded by people who contribute to the problem, but it's the most rewarding effort you can make. Great things happen when people choose to be part of the solution. What's your choice?

EXCEPTIONALIZE IT!™

Contribute to the solution.
Reject participation
in and propagation
of the problem.

Are You Stuck in Old Behaviors?

To deliver exceptional performance in the future, you need to recognize that, until now, you did not deliver it. It requires the admission that whatever you have done so far was not exceptional. It's a humbling moment to recognize and admit that. After all, you thought you were doing your best. However, this critical moment of recognition is essential to starting anew. Your old performance came with some old behaviors. These were the behaviors that shaped the quality of your performance. They led you to the average results that came with average efforts that failed to impress your customers and colleagues. It's time to let go of those old habits. Whatever your old tricks and techniques were, they didn't get you as far as exceptional. It's time to look for new behaviors.

When we talk about old habits and behaviors, they run the gamut from choice of language to the amount of time you invest to create your performance. It is time to reexamine them all. Do you invest the right amount of time to exceed customers' expectations? Do you research and prepare yourself for each interaction? Do you choose your words carefully to create emotional engagement? Do you pay attention to personal cues from your customers and act on them?

In the past, your behaviors didn't support exceptional performance. It's time to let them go. It's time to realize that behind the meta-decision to deliver exceptional performance is set of small decisions to let go of old behaviors and introduce and practice new behaviors.

EXCEPTIONALIZE IT!™

Which of your old behaviors do you need to let go?

Trust Me

What do you do when you hear someone say, "Trust me"?
Well, if you're like most people, you do exactly the opposite of
trusting that person. After all, why does he need to ask for your
trust? The same is true when, in the middle of a conversation,
you hear the famous statement, "To be honest with you...."
Well, what were you doing until now, lying? These common
statements evoke exactly the opposite of the intended message.
They cause you to rethink your colleagues' trust and honesty.

These are typical examples of old habits we need to let go if
we want to deliver exceptional performance. These comments
are so ingrained in our behavior that we say them without
thinking. They evoke the opposite of what we are trying
to convey. Rethink your choice of words, analogies, and
expressions. Words are powerful tools to evoke customer
connection. Our words tell the whole story about who we
are, our intentions, and our relationships. Trustworthy people
don't need to say they're trustworthy. Their actions and
reputation speak louder and more convincingly than their
words. Let go of the old habits of promising trust and honesty.
Adopt new behaviors that demonstrate you are a trustworthy
person.

EXCEPTIONALIZE IT!™

Your actions, not your promises, should establish your trustworthiness.

Challenge Your Assumptions

In 2004 the world's largest social network was launched. It was called Orkut. It was so successful it almost crushed its operator's servers. But it wasn't developed further, opening the doors for Facebook to emerge and lead the market. Orkut's owner: Google. The reason it languishes: Google's old assumptions. Google built its success on its superior algorithms. As such the company could not envision rankings based on people's opinion, which was the logic behind Orkut and the concept of social networks. Google let its old assumptions dictate its future. Orkut ended up leading the social media in Brazil, where it is currently located, but left the rest of the world to the dominance of Facebook.

If it happened to Google it could happen to anyone. Old assumptions are our comfort zone. They are what brought us to our current success. New assumptions are risky and unfamiliar. Reexamine your old assumptions. Don't restrict yourself to old thinking. Make sure that success doesn't fill your mind to the point that you're not open anymore. Keep an open mind to the future and embrace the new assumptions that it may bring with it.

EXCEPTIONALIZE IT!™

How often do you open
yourself up to new ideas
and challenge your
assumptions?

The Power I Don't Have
Versus The Power I Do Have

How much power do you have to delight customers?
Well, it depends. I'm sure you can see yourself with more
power. Even the CEO of GE can imagine more power if the
board of directors will only let go a bit. Every employee or
executive has limitations. Every role has its limitations. Every
task has it boundaries. Every employee, no matter how high up
he is in the organization, has limitations. Limitations may be
in the form of budget, resources, time, attention, knowledge,
or any other power you may need. The question is: where do
you turn your focus? Do you focus on the power you don't
have or the power you do have? Do you focus on the budget,
resources, and knowledge you do have or keep on excusing
your performance because of the power you don't have?

In the realm of challenges you face, you have power, resources,
budget, time, and knowledge to impact the customer. Think
creatively and you will discover new ways to leverage the
power you do have to *Exceptionalize It!* Stop focusing on what
you're not allowed to do and start focusing on the power you
do have and you'll start to amaze your customers and yourself.

EXCEPTIONALIZE IT!™

Stop excusing
your performance.
Leverage all the power
you do have.

Multiply Your Power

If you decided to lead and not wait for the committee, now is time to create momentum. You can leverage all the power you have to make a difference in the lives of many customers. Or you can enlist the network of people you work with and leverage their power to impact even more customers. Everyone has a set of resources they can use to delight customers. Start with a smile and a positive attitude and you'll make progress; leverage the people around and you'll multiply the impact.

If you start your mini-revolution, people will join. People will join authentic efforts and passionate people. I once worked with a brand where a general manager had approached me to assist the company in creating exceptional experiences for its customers. What started as a single person's initiative grew quickly into a 100-volunteer effort, which enabled him to launch a nationwide event tour in a record 51 days. People believed in his vision and were attracted to his passion and they were all willing to join forces to make it a reality.

Share your vision and passion, chart a way forward, and then invite others to join you. Together you can achieve more, and do it faster than you can alone. Allow others to share your mission. Share the opportunity to impact people.

EXCEPTIONALIZE IT!™

Multiply your efforts by enlisting volunteers.

Impact Performance Versus Functional Performance

Let's assume for a moment that you manufacture candles. What are candles? They are a wick and solid form of oil. Or are they? If you view your work as a functional performance, this will be an accurate depiction of your work. If you view the candle from the perspective of the customer, you will discover that you are not in the candle business. You are in fact in the party and celebration business or the decoration business or the comfort business. From the usage perspective, a candle is a ray of light, a symbol of celebration, a decoration, or a comforting flame for the bereaved.

Viewing your work from a strictly functional perspective will wear you down and burn you out. Instead, connecting to the people who use your work to brighten their life will brighten yours as well. It will provide you with a clear sense of power and mission. This is impact performance.

Now let's review the past 90 days of staff meetings. How much time did you dedicate to discussing with your colleagues the virtues of their work and how it impacts customers? How often did you discuss with your colleagues the power they have to impact customers? Most managers focus their staff meetings on the functional aspects of the work. They have to-do lists and assignments. But they fail to create a line of sight to the real impact employees' performance is making on real people. It's time to provide your colleagues and employees with the gift of power by discussing with them the impact their performance makes.

EXCEPTIONALIZE IT!™

Do you know what
impact your performance
has on customers?

Are You Relevant?

Even the most expensive watch (and some of them are sold for $250,000 or more) will become useless if it doesn't keep time. It may become an object of aesthetics, but it is not relevant as a watch. The same is applicable to our performance.

If we continue to deliver yesterday's performance and don't evolve with time, we lose relevance. What was amazing yesterday is today's common sense. What was surprising yesterday is taken for granted today and will be old news tomorrow.

Keep on evolving. Keep on innovating your performance. Don't settle for yesterday's exceptionalism. Be the first one to create a new standard for exceptionalism. Be relevant today.

EXCEPTIONALIZE IT!™

Are you delivering
today's exceptionalism,
or merely copying
yesterday's performance?

Stop Averaging

When you deliver average performance, you think you fit in the middle of the acceptable performance chart. In reality, average is the place no one remembers. Do you remember the team that finished 8th in the NBA 2010/2011 season? Of course not. Everyone focuses on the number one team and players.

Just because average is a possible outcome doesn't mean you should strive for it. In fact, you should never accept it as your standard. Average belongs to those people who want to be forgotten. Average is a form of quitting (while trying hard not to get fired).

If you already perform at the average, go for the only place that matters: the top spot. Set your own standards. Establish a goal you will be proud to achieve.

EXCEPTIONALIZE IT!™

Stop being average
and start setting your
own high standards.

You Are Entitled to Nothing

All the problems start when you feel you're entitled to something you didn't earn. A sense of entitlement distorts your perception. Instead of working to achieve your dreams, you try to reach them through handouts. History shows us that most true top achievers didn't get anything for free that helped them achieve their goals. They didn't get anything for free from their parents, bosses, or government. They worked for their achievements.

The most successful leaders don't approach life with an attitude of entitlement. The faster we shed our sense of entitlement, the faster we will be ready to start fulfilling our dreams. Delivering exceptional performance requires us to accept the customer as the ultimate judge of that performance. Creating exceptional performance that will impress customers is dependent on our ability to accept that we are not entitled to anything from our customers and therefore need to work for their acceptance and appreciation.

EXCEPTIONALIZE IT!™

Entitlement is an obstacle to reaching exceptional performance.

The World Belongs to Those Who Earn It

The world belongs to those individuals who make sacrifices to earn the right to live their dreams. For those who *Exceptionalize It!*, exceptionalism is not a quick fix. Exceptional performance requires determination, conscious decisions, and the discipline of follow through.

What are you willing to sacrifice for exceptionalism? This is the core question each and every one of us needs to confront. Claiming entitlement will not get you anywhere close to your dreams. Working hard and earning it will. The potential to *Exceptionalize It!* is inside each and every one of us. Those who fulfilled their potential for exceptionalism did so by making sacrifices and trading off short-term enjoyment for long-term impact.

EXCEPTIONALIZE IT!™

Are you ready
to earn your
exceptionalism?

The Race Is On

The question of being exceptional is not a philosophical one. This is not a debate about whether delivering exceptional performance is the right way to go. In today's competitive environment, exceptional performance is not an option. It is a matter of surviving and, more importantly, thriving.

Moreover, the question is not *whether* we should *Exceptionalize It!* but rather, will we win the race to do it. It is a question of execution. The outcome will be determined by who will lead, who will execute on exceptional performance across the whole organization, and who will reach the highest in terms of delighting customers and surprising them with exceptional experiences. The race is on. You had better be part of it. The time for debate is over.

EXCEPTIONALIZE IT!™

The race for exceptional
performance is on.
Are you in?

♥

MANAGER

The Employee Choice

We recently surveyed one client's customers and presented them with 29 different customer experience drivers to rank. Although "knowing me as a person" and "delivering great value" were among those 29 different factors, employees' pride and passion led the list of customers' top loyalty drivers. Basically, customers stated that dealing with passionate people who are proud of their work creates the difference that brings them back. The problem with that is you can't pay people to be proud or passionate.

In a product-centric world, we need employees who follow procedures and processes. In a customer-powered world, we need engaged employees who demonstrate pride and passion. However, demonstrating these is a personal choice made by each employee. No traditional management tool can elicit it.

A brand or a company's real value is the sum total of its employees' choices. If employees choose to delight customers, the brand will be strong and profitable. If employees choose otherwise, the financial results will be disappointing. Let me illustrate this point. The average contact center employee takes 10,000 calls a year. These are 10,000 opportunities to delight customers or destroy loyalty. Each employee's choice will determine the future spend of the customers they interact with. Today, more than ever before, managers and organizations are highly dependent on the personal choice of every employee about whether to delight customers or destroy loyalty.

EXCEPTIONALIZE IT!™

What choices do your employees make?

Employees' Pride and Passion Above All

Most companies take employees' pride and passion for granted. Executives assume that their employees are naturally passionate and proud. This is a false assumption. As a result, the investment in developing and maintaining pride and employee passion receives little attention in corporate investment. There is more budget allocated to employees' technologies, tools, and process training than to employees' pride in the brand. Yet much of what is needed to foster employees' pride and passion takes more personal investment than hard dollars.

Start with demonstrating passion for what *you* do, and for the company. Make it authentic by hiring people who actually love what *they* do, and what the company does and what it stands for. Look for people who are inspired by helping others and then keep the momentum going by nurturing the pride. Employees' passion and pride plays a crucial role in your ability to connect to customers.

EXCEPTIONALIZE IT!™

Dedicate the time and resources to nurture employees' passion *every day!*

The Daily Choice: Excellence or Mediocrity

Every day when your employees enter the office they have a choice to make. Will they deliver excellence or mediocrity today? If they are ready and willing to make the choice for excellence, you will *Exceptionalize It!* If not, you are doomed to boring your customers. This is the daily choice that determines your differentiation. It is this choice that drives customer choice. Your employees need to make this choice every day. As the adage goes, you are only as strong as your weakest link. In the case of exceptionalism, the weakest link is the employee who choses mediocrity.

Take the number of employees you have and multiply it by the number of work days in a year then multiply it by the number of interactions they conduct every day and you can see how many choices need to be made to raise your organization to the level of excellence you strive to achieve. Your value is the sum total of these choices multiplied by the number of interactions an employee has every day.

Employees are well trained to follow procedures and processes. But to *Exceptionalize It!* this requires a personal choice they and only they can make. Although you can't order this choice to be made, you can build and nurture an environment that will entice employees to make the daily choice for excellence.

How many employees made the choice for excellence today? Why did they make that choice? How can you encourage more employees to choose excellence? These are the questions every leader must ask. As leader, your role is to create the environment that will encourage employees to choose excellence every day.

EXCEPTIONALIZE IT!™

What have you done today
to invite employees to
choose excellence?

Welcome to "Generation Why?"

You know them when you see them. They bear special characteristics in the workplace and in life. They are known as Generation Y. The Millennial generation arrived at the workplace with Internet savvy and with a strong sense of entitlement. Business leaders around the world are seeking creative ways to manage, engage, and motivate this new generation of workers. These employees seem to operate by a different code of ethics.

I would like to propose a slight tweak to the definition of the problem that will shed light on how managers can resolve it. Let's switch their nickname to Generation Why. By doing so, we're going to the heart of these employees' challenge. They're not good at following orders, nor are they willingly to accept top-down instructions. They are asking *why?* The dialogue with them must change to include the logic behind the projects and work. They need to know why and, more importantly, understand the impact it will make on the world before they decide to participate. Focusing the organization on the customer will establish a solid foundation to answer the question *why?*

By changing the name from Gen Y to Gen Why, we actually expand this employee group to include many of the cynics in your office who seem disengaged. They are usually disengaged because they no longer know why they do what they do. Having a strong answer to *why?* will be a powerful motivator to both the Millennial employees and the cynics.

Many managers will find it threatening to need to explain *why*. Their bosses never needed to do so. Why should they? Well, welcome to the new reality. If you want your employees engaged, start changing the dialogue. Start talking about the why and connect your employees to a meaningful mission, like the power you have to solve people's problems and make their lives better. Now *that* will make people get up an hour early to change the world.

EXCEPTIONALIZE IT!™

Processes are important,
but only explaining *why* will
deliver exceptional results.

Your Employees Mirror You

Want to know why your employees don't deliver exceptional performance? Start by looking in the mirror. Your employees' performance mirrors yours. They follow your lead. If you play the blame game, they will do the same. If you take initiative, they will follow your lead and do the same. Employees live in the comfort zone of reflecting their manager's behavior. They assume that the behavior delivered by the manager is the safe modus operandi.

When you expect your employees to deliver exceptional performance, ask yourself several simple questions. What exceptional performance have I delivered recently? How often do I venture into exceptional performance? Is it the rule or the exception to the rule?

Make the choice to deliver exceptional performance, and your employees will follow.

EXCEPTIONALIZE IT!™

What exceptional performance have you delivered today?

Do You Trust Your Employees?

Much has been written about the importance of empowering employees. Customers don't want to do business with employees who lack the authority to solve their problems. If you are the ultimate decision maker, then your employee is redundant. To *Exceptionalize It!* you need to give your employees the power to deliver on the spot: the power to solve problems, close the deal, or do whatever it takes to delight the customer.

Many managers believe that they empower their employees, but within reason. They trust them only 50% of the time. There is no such thing as 50% trust. You either trust your employees or you don't. So take the time to reflect and determine the answer to this question: do you trust your employees?

If you don't trust them, they have no place in your organization. They definitely have no place facing your customers—especially if you're trying to *Exceptionalize It!* If you do trust your employees, then take the time to provide them with the knowledge and training to deliver exceptional performance to your customers.

EXCEPTIONALIZE IT!™

Trust your employees, and make sure you demonstrate that trust.

Are All Employees Lazy?

Are all your employees lazy or are they hard-working people? Well, here we are again with the famous, "It depends." No, it doesn't. If you believe you have employees who will become lazy unless you work them hard and keep them on a tight leash, you either hired the wrong people or you failed to motivate them with the purpose of their work.

Here again you will counter-argue with a horror story from 1987 when management discovered that one employee was regularly playing golf on his own instead of with the clients he was supposed to be entertaining, and therefore you need to "plug all the holes." The issue is not the "hole plugging." The issue is with your perspective. If deep down you believe that all employees are lazy unless proven otherwise, your actions will follow this conviction. You will not respect them and allow them the freedom to perform to their highest level of exceptionalism. You will instead, micro-manage them to no end and wear them out and kill every ounce of their motivation and commitment.

Rethink your convictions. Don't lead your people based on the lowest common denominator of a few employees' performance. And don't design the rules based on those few. Address those employees as the exception to the rule.

EXCEPTIONALIZE IT!™

Design your employee engagement based on trust. Address the few outliers as the exceptions, not as the rule.

Cynicism Hurts… Your Bottom Line

Cynicism is not an individual problem. It has a direct impact on your ability to achieve your corporate goals. It seems harmless, but in reality it siphons productivity and morale out of your employees and in the process kills innovation, customer experience, employee engagement, and ultimately profits.

It all starts with one cynical joke made by a manager who feels helpless and hopeless and expresses his frustration to everyone in the organization. The joke starts to travel and by the end of the day infects hundreds, if not thousands, of employees in the company. Now they all have the bug. They are suffering from organizational mistrust. Skepticism starts creeping in and takes their performance hostage. They start to adopt the mind-set of "why bother?" or "no one really cares." Their performance follows.

Instead of owning the customer problem and solving it, these demotivated employees give away freebies and waive payments. Instead of demonstrating the unique value (which they believe is not unique) they offer greater discounts. Instead of promoting a new product, they insist on selling the old ones. "Our customers don't need the new features," they argue. The illness of organizational cynicism is now translating into a hard cold reality that impacts your revenues and profits.

As a manger, you need to recognize cynicism's damaging impact on your employees and on your results. Countering cynicism must be on your agenda. Do not ignore it. Cynicism will not self-correct. It will not go away.

EXCEPTIONALIZE IT!™

Put cynicism
on your agenda.
It is a serious cause of
organizational damage.
Act on It.

Put the Soul in the Organization, Not on the Wall

Every company I've had the privilege of working with has had an inspiring vision and mission statement. As I worked with them I noticed an interesting dichotomy. Those companies that had their visions brashly displayed on the wall usually had little action behind it. Those companies that displayed their visions more subtly on their walls had employees who followed and fulfilled those missions. I didn't do a scientific assessment of this phenomenon. My experience, however, has been that those who brazenly displayed their missions on the wall did so to cover up for the lack of actually living by the mission. They thought that loud displays could disguise the cynical approach in their daily operation. Their employees viewed those signs as disingenuous.

On the contrary, those companies that did not use loud, flashy displays to express their mission and values did better in delivering them. The executives at these companies focused on placing the mission in employees' souls more than on the building's walls. They invested in reinforcement of the values and mission through ongoing training, staff meetings, town halls, and role modeling. They ensured that employees were not cynical, but rather inspired by the mission. The companies also ensured that employees don't have obstacles stopping them from fulfilling the mission.

Mission and values are not signs on the wall, they are a living operation. They come to life through people's actions. They are self-evident. Most of all, they require ongoing investment in ensuring they are alive and inspiring your employees. When it comes to your company's mission and vision, you must place it in employees' souls, not display it on the walls.

EXCEPTIONALIZE IT!™

Where does your mission
and vision reside, on
the corporate walls or in
employees' souls?

You Can't Pay Employees to Smile Sincerely

A paycheck only goes so far. It can buy employees' attendance, but it cannot buy exceptional performance. Smiling sincerely is one of those exceptional performance characteristics that require special nurturing. It joins other qualities of exceptional performance, such as caring, sincerity, integrity, risk taking, decision-making, creativity, and leadership that you cannot mandate from the top. Every time an employee is forced to smile, it will look forced and unconvincing. More importantly, instead of engaging customers and building loyalty, it will have the opposite effect: it will drive customers away.

Smiling sincerely is a matter of a personal choice. Every employee must choose to produce an authentic smile that will engage customers. The same logic is applicable to delivering exceptional performance. Exceptional performance is outside of traditional management tools and requires a new way to engage, court, and persuade an employee to bring his exceptional game to every customer interaction.

Managers can't force exceptional performance any more than they can force an authentic smile. They can invite employees to join and participate. They can create a natural environment that will make exceptional performance a natural choice for their employees.

EXCEPTIONALIZE IT!™

Does your management style invite employees to deliver exceptional performance?

The Growth Manager

What do your employees aspire to achieve in their lives? What are their dreams? What new skills do they want to learn? What new experiences do they want to try? Welcome to your real role: The Growth Manager.

The ultimate motivator of employees is not money (they will always aspire for more; no one feels they have enough). The ultimate motivator is a sense of growth; the sense of learning something new and trying new things. Your employees aspire to grow and be better off than yesterday in both their personal and professional lives. Are you ready to assume your role as chief coach, inspirer, and growth manager? If you wish to unleash the power of your employees' performance, you need to assume the role of the growth manager.

In a disciplined way, you need to discover and document your employees' aspirations and develop a growth plan for each. When your employees see you as their chief coach and the provider of their goal-fulfillment, they will follow your leadership and help you achieve your goals, as well.

EXCEPTIONALIZE IT!™

Develop the discipline to grow your people.

Give Me a Cause to Volunteer For

The phenomenon is universal. Wherever you have a cause you'll get volunteers. When the founder of Linux, the alternative operating system to Microsoft Windows, started to develop his new invention, he had no money or structure. All he had was a cause. The rest worked like magic. Thousands of software developers, who usually get paid handsomely for their advanced skills, volunteered their time and creativity to develop Linux. They believed in the cause of providing alternative solutions and giving customers a choice.

Always present a challenge to your employees as an opportunity to make a difference. A cause is an opportunity for your employees to feel powerful. It focuses on the power they do have and helps to make their work meaningful. Adding value to stockholders is not an appealing cause. Making people's lives better will inspire employees.
Transform your projects into causes and tap into the spirit of volunteering in your employees.

EXCEPTIONALIZE IT!™

What difference can
your employees make
in your customers' lives?

Employees Choices = Profitability

Let's imagine that you're managing a restaurant and your dishwasher is in a bad mood today. As a result, he defaulted to mediocrity instead of choosing excellence. The wine glasses he washed were full of spots. Your guests received spotty glasses and many sent them back to the kitchen. As a result you had to replace the glasses of wine at your expense. What started as a moody dishwasher ended up with several bottles of wine that were wasted to compensate your customers. (Please note that the dishwasher never saw a single guest, and yet he was able to destroy satisfaction, loyalty, and profit margins by a simple choice.)

Every employee action and interaction makes an impact on the customer. When your employees don't choose excellence, you will end up paying the price. Conversely, when your employees choose to exceptionalize their performance, you will end up reaping the profits. Ultimately, customers pay for what they get. If they receive an average experience, they will take action that adjusts their payment accordingly. If the experience is exceptional, they will adjust their financial reward accordingly.

If you seek to maximize your customer relationships, loyalty, and profits, you must *Exceptionalize It!* This is not optional. Your employees' every day choices drive your top-line revenues and your bottom-line profitability. Investing in your employees' choices is the best assurance to maximizing results.

EXCEPTIONALIZE IT!™

Inspire employees to choose excellence daily.

SUCCESS

The Success Trap

The most dangerous part of every business is success. Success breeds complacency. Success turns you from a ready-to-delight person to a ready-to-enjoy person. You treat success as "cash-out time" and that's when you start slipping. That's when you begin to take things for granted and assume you've discovered an eternal formula for success. In reality, your competitors are already working on plans to topple your success. They noticed it, they're copying it, and they're trying to do it better and bolder than you. While you enjoy a celebratory glass of champagne they're working on your demise.

Success transforms your mind-set. It makes you believe in your success as a guarantee for the future. There are no guarantees. The success trap is the attempt to continue to do what worked in the past and not evolve. It's the loss of hunger; succumbing to incremental corrections as opposed to bolder exceptionalism. For a period of time, your success formula will carry you. You will repeat the past and customers will pay for it. But, eventually, they will get bored. Your competitors will reinvent themselves and you will still be repeating the past.

Beware of the success trap. Do not fall into the calming assumption that past success is an indication of the future. Go on the offensive and search for the next bold thing that will surprise your customers.

EXCEPTIONALIZE IT!™

Success is a trap.
Past success is not a
guaranteed formula
for the future.

Number One Is a One-Time Achievement

Here you are. You've made it. You climbed the business version of Everest and you reached the peak, the view is amazing. Now what? Once organizations strive to be number one and achieve their goal, they discover a simple truth: they have nothing more to strive for. So, they switch to a defensive strategy to retain the position.

Smart organizations don't set a single-peak goal like being number one. They design a multi-peak goal that will challenge them in the future. They focus on being a pioneer, not a number one player. Number one players compare themselves to their mediocre competitors. Pioneers compare themselves against their future and new possibilities. Pioneers challenge themselves; they don't wait for their competitors to present a threat. Pioneers are those who chart a new path, beyond one charted by the traditional competition. They define their own road to continued and greater success.

EXCEPTIONALIZE IT!™

Pioneer a new path.
Don't accept number one
as the place to be.

Are You Open?

Business leaders at startups and young companies are often open to new ideas. They tend to listen carefully and stay flexible. They do whatever it takes to delight customers. Customers, in turn, love the flexibility and reward these eager-to-please companies with more business and referrals. These organizations are the exact opposite of their more established competitors, which provide little flexibility to their customers. Openness and flexibility provide the competitive edge for small and young companies.

As these businesses grow, they become busy and, as a result, become less and less flexible and open. The same secret for success that made these companies successful quickly evaporates and turns them into exactly what customers didn't like in the more established providers. These agile businesses become an exact copy of the competitors their customers left. They lose their edge.

Openness and flexibility are what allow you to create experiences that are intimate and suitable to your customers. These attributes are the way you fit yourself to your customers rather than forcing them to fit to your business processes. Don't lose your openness. Always keep your ears and eyes open for the changing trends and tastes of your customers, and stay flexible enough to react to them. Retain your sense of discovery; be willing to change. Dedicate time and resources to openness and flexibility.

EXCEPTIONALIZE IT!™

Stay open to new ideas and be flexible enough to adapt to them.

Busy With Business

When we become successful, our organization grows and, with growth, comes a new layer of bureaucracy. How many conference calls do you participate in without being sure why you're there? How many emails (especially those with a 10 GB presentation attached) are you copied on even though you have no real contribution to the discussion? How many meetings did you attend without adding a single word to the conversation? These invitations are all made with a great deal of respect to you, but, in the process you are robbed of precious time you need to focus on your customers and add value to them.

Success breeds growth, but large organizations become enamored with the culture of business. The larger the organization, the greater the amount of time dedicated to internal meetings and interaction. As a result, there is less time available to create exceptionalism that will win the race for success. Internal coordination soaks up efforts and resources at the expense of creating new values for customers.

This addiction to inclusion for the sake of inclusion must stop. It's a waste of precious time that results in incremental benefits at best. Free up your time. The emails can wait. Create quiet time when your email is shut down. Inform people to exclude you from simple FYI correspondence. Only attend conference calls and meetings that are relevant and that you will actively contribute to. Dedicate the majority of your time to creation, not attendance.

EXCEPTIONALIZE IT!™

Free up your time to create exceptional performance.

Ego Is a Great Way to Get Lost

Another typical byproduct of success is ego. We start the journey with a humble approach honoring the privilege to serve customers. Every customer is precious at that early stage in success, but then success brings more customers—and with them a notion of "I did it," "I am invincible," and "I know better than anyone else."

Think for a moment. Who comes first, you or your customer? Listen to your ego and it will tell you to focus on yourself first. The truth is that ego is nothing more than a self-centric compass. It will twist everything to be all about you. Listen to your ego, be self-centric, and you will never notice anyone else. The ego as a compass will not lead you to success, but will get you lost instead.

Delivering exceptional performance requires the humility to accept the needs of others, often before your own. It requires you to see yourself as a vehicle for giving. Your needs will be fulfilled by the fulfillment of others' needs. This attitude of servitude that is required for exceptional performance is in direct conflict with the ego. We are all here to serve customers. They pay the bills and therefore come first.

If you want to reach your highest level of performance–to *Exceptionalize It!*–you will need to focus on others and not just yourself. You will need to see others as the canvas on which you will paint your best masterpiece. Let your ego go so you can let your talent fly.

EXCEPTIONALIZE IT!™

Let go of your ego
and focus on
others' needs.

The Shrinking Time of Success

Right before the holiday shopping season several years ago, Apple announced the next version of the iPod. The world was waiting for the next big innovation. Instead, Steve Jobs announced that the next generation iPod would come in a variety of colors. It wasn't exactly big news, but it was critical for Apple. Many innovators know that the length of time for enjoying success is continuing to diminish.

Success used to last for years; today it is merely days before someone else will outdo your great idea. Celebrate your success. Don't ignore it. But then move on quickly. Somewhere in the world there is an innovator who is looking to create the next big thing that will make your great success yesterday's news.

We live in a time where success is ever-shrinking. Today's innovation is tomorrow's boredom. Innovation is no longer a defined event or activity, but rather an ongoing way of life. You can no longer be a "one trick pony." You now need to reinvent yourself every day. Don't let success blind you from the need to evolve. Live an innovative life and never get complacent.

EXCEPTIONALIZE IT!™

Do you live a life of innovation?

Innovation Everywhere

When we think about innovation we often associate it with white-lab-coat-wearing scientists or nerdy technologists working on the next big thing. Product-centric organizations are focused on waiting for the big breakthrough that will come from the lab. In the customer-empowered economy, we can no longer wait for that one big breakthrough. Creating exceptional experiences is about creating breakthroughs every day for every customer. Innovations need to redefine things that every employee does every day in every action.

We need to define and foster innovation differently and unleash the imagination and creative power of our people. From website design to process design to the way we solve customer problems, all are opportunities to innovate. Writing terms-and-conditions documents that treat the customer with respect and speak a simple language is an example of an easy, yet impactful, innovation. Innovation must occupy every aspect of the customer journey. It needs to be an integral part of every interaction with customers. Employees need to know that innovation is in the small, every day actions. These innovations need to be embraced and practiced by all. Your organization is the sum total of the innovative and creative actions of all your people.

EXCEPTIONALIZE IT!™

Unleash the power of imagination and creativity in all your employees.

Creator, Not Consumer

Today's customer is no longer just a consumer. He can be an author, an actor, a designer, a newscaster, or a merchant all at the click of a button. They have vast power to create their own products and express their own viewpoints publicly. This has changed the customer forever. Customers have evolved from consumers of predefined products and services to creators. Customers are designers looking for tools and inspiration to express their own vision.

Organizations must evolve accordingly. In the past, companies "owned" all the ideas. Now we need to accept the humble position that companies are no longer the only designers in town. Consumers are no longer passive recipients who pay for cool ideas and relevant products. Today's customers seek tools and platforms to express themselves. Companies need to evolve their brands from being a destination to being a platform that encourages customers to share ideas, co-create products, and express their individuality.

Vendors that embrace their new role as the provider of platforms, inspiration, and tools to support customers' creativity will win the hearts and wallets of customers. Accepting the customer as an equal creator will hold the key to your future success.

EXCEPTIONALIZE IT!™

Provide your
customer-creator
with the inspiration
and tools to succeed.

Fringe Behavior Is Where the Future May Come From

You know these customers. You consider them annoying because they always ask you for one-off solutions that no other customers have ever asked for. They are the fringe-behavior customers. Their requests always require special changes to address their unique needs. And, you go through those special needs you wonder, "Why can't they be like everyone else?"

When Nike noticed the "Pimp Your Nike" ads on Craigslist, they probably had similar thoughts. Instead of dismissing these one-off customers, the company decided to embrace them. It took a cue from these ads and developed NikeId.com, a website dedicated to empowering customers to design their own Nike shoes. Instead of dismissing fringe customers, Nike made them mainstream and developed a whole new line of business with higher profitability. The company didn't argue with its customers; instead it profited from their creativity.

Product-centric companies find fringe requests an annoyance. Customer-centric companies view them as unmet needs that should be addressed. Don't dismiss your fringe customers. Redesign your future for them.

EXCEPTIONALIZE IT!™

What idea did you get today from a fringe customer?

Fail Professionally

Failure is part of life and it's a part of learning. However, most executives and organizations don't know how to fail. I recall a comment during a focus group when an employee shared with me, "In our company, we are all empowered to make the right decisions." How ironic. There is no such thing. Yet, organizations send a clear message: make the right decision and you're in. Make the wrong the decision and you're out. This is the equivalent of a baseball coach telling his players, "If it's not a home run don't bother coming back to the dugout. You're fired."

Even the best baseball player will strike out 65 percent of the time. Does that mean he stops swinging? No, that would be disastrous. Swinging is part of training to succeed and thus an integral part of success. Not taking the risk is the mistake and the failure. We need to adopt the same approach in the workplace. Not making decisions or taking calculated risks, not failing, is the ultimate failure. It's paralyzing to the organization. Failure is an integral part of success. It's the training every employee must take to get to a professional home run.

We need to create an environment in which failures are positive; where there are trials and errors on the path to discovery. Discovery will never take place unless someone tries. We need to celebrate the trials and initiatives, as well as create a reward system for those who are willing to try. They are the ones who will lead us to the next big thing.

EXCEPTIONALIZE IT!™

How do you celebrate failures?

Passion: Keep It Relevant and Alive

How important is passion to success? It is one of those invisible ingredients. You can't really define it, but you know it when you see it. It makes a huge difference when you experience it. Your customers will gravitate to passion. They will feel the warmth and caring from the special attitude that emanates from passionate employees. They will want to be part of it.

Passion is the secret sauce that helps many employees and organizations achieve success. Unlike secret sauces that are designed once and applied repeatedly, passion is different because it requires constant remixing and reenergizing. To stay fresh, authentic, and relevant, passion needs to be refueled.

Plan and dedicate time to recharge your passion and your employees' passion. Remember, the passion is what got you where you are. It is what customers gravitated to. Keep it alive. It is too easy to fall into a routine and repeat past performance. When you get jaded, customers feel that your heart is no longer there.

Reenergize and renew your passion every day. You owe it to your customers and employees. You owe it to your future success. Most importantly, you owe it to yourself.

EXCEPTIONALIZE IT!™

Grow and nurture your passion.

Pride in Making a Difference

What are you most proud of at work? Making money? Closing deals? Completing tasks? If you ask employees they will tell you that they draw pride from the opportunity to make a difference. How do they make a difference? By helping other people, whether assisting internal colleagues or external customers, the power to be in a position to help others is often the source of employees' pride.

The pride in what your brand represents and, more importantly, in what it delivers every day to your customers, should be at the top of your agenda. If your employees are proud of that, they will find the energy, resources, and creativity to do whatever it takes to get the job done and *Exceptionalize It!* for customers.

Pride in the brand is not inhaled from the air at your offices. Pride needs to be instilled. You need to develop and deliver dedicated messages and content to reinforce the real purpose of your brand's existence. You need to demonstrate how to deliver on the brand promise and make a difference in customers' lives. This doesn't mean running a flowery ad campaign. It means communicating and demonstrating to employees how meaningful their work is. It's about charging them with the energy to go and reach the next peak or create the next innovation.

Like passion, pride in the brand attracts customers. They like to do business with people who are proud of what they do. Such authentic pride is usually the territory of small organizations. It is the competitive advantage of entrepreneurs, who are often very close to their customers and can demonstrate it naturally. When employees are empowered to help customers, they too will show authentic pride. But remember, for pride to develop, employees must see how you deliver on your brand promise, not just how you advertise it.

EXCEPTIONALIZE IT!™

Pride in your brand
must be instilled in
every employee on
an ongoing basis.

Color Your World With Customers

Look around your office, your conference rooms, and your hallways. What decorates your walls? Are your walls full of photographs of your products? Are they decorated with a framed copy of the corporate mission statement, the founder's pictures, and signs of your strengths? Or, maybe there's a map of your branches around the world or images of your factories and trucks? If the answer is yes, it's time to redecorate.

Why aren't images of customers and testimonials the focal point of your corporate visuals? What message does it send to your employees and to yourself? We decorate our walls with what we value. If your walls are full of your corporate images, the message is quite clear: It's all about us. You are saying, "Customers are merely tools to achieve our own goals."

If customers are the focal point of your strategy and operation, put them on the wall. Color your world with images of your customers. Send a clear message to everyone about where they should focus their efforts. It's not difficult to do, yet the vast majority of companies don't do it. They love dressing up in their own colors. It is a mind-set. The images we select to decorate our business tell our story. So tell a customer story, not a self-centric story. Remember that your products and services are nothing more than vehicles to achieve memorable experiences for customers. What the products and services do for the customers is what really matters. Capture those images and remind yourself and your organization of what you're all about.

EXCEPTIONALIZE IT!™

Focus on what matters. Decorate your business life with images of customers.

Are There Butterflies in Your Stomach?

Success brings with it a routine. If you act like you have discovered the formula, now all you do is simply repeat yourself. If it isn't broken, don't fix it, the adage says. In the process of repeating the same actions and processes that led to your current success, you lose the butterflies in your stomach. You lose that special sense of discovery and anticipation for the future. Well, don't. Don't ever lose those butterflies.

It was actually those butterflies—the fear of failure and making mistakes—that kept you going. They were the power that challenged you to try harder, reach higher, and get better. Lose them and you lose the engine that moved you.

Challenge yourself. Identify the next peak that will present an opportunity for growth and excitement. Set a new goal that will inspire you to make sacrifices, learn new things, and create new opportunities. Keep the butterflies alive. They're not a sign of weakness. They're your badge of strength.

EXCEPTIONALIZE IT!™

Power your success with butterflies.

Exceptionalism:
The Ultimate Measure of Success

By now you know that delivering exceptional performance is the way forward. Hopefully, you've gained insight into what to do and what to stop doing to *Exceptionalize It!* The race is on. Excuses will not help. Ego will be an unnecessary blinder. It is time to raise your sights to the highest bar and beyond. There is only one question left: Are you exceptional?

I can't answer this question for you. Only you and your customers can. You have to ask this question tomorrow and the next day, and the next week, and months and years ahead. You need to ask yourself whether you *Exceptionalize It!* every day.

You also need to look to your customers to determine whether you're exceptionalizing it. Their actions will be the ultimate measure. Exceptional experiences command premium prices. If your customers refuse to pay a premium, your performance is not exceptional. But if you think you're delivering exceptional performance to customers who aren't willing to reciprocate by paying a premium price, then you're doing business with the wrong customers. It is as simple as that.

Investors don't want you to waste your profits on providing exceptional experiences to unprofitable customers. Profitable customers want you to reinvest in them, not in unprofitable customers. Customers expect you to invest your profits in reinventing your performance and ensuring that the exceptionalism they've experienced with you will remain for the long term. Paying a premium price is an investment in relationships, not a subsidy for other customers who won't pay for the value they receive. (They will consider your use of their profits to delight others as a form of betrayal.)

Focus on the profitability of individual customers as the indicator of the health of your customer relationships. It's an indication that you're focusing on the right customers who appreciate your exceptional performance, and who are willing to reward it accordingly.

EXCEPTIONALIZE IT!™

Profitability is the proof
that your customers
appreciate your
exceptional performance.

Be All In

In Las Vegas there's a moment that changes everything. It's when a player goes all in. He puts in all of his chips as his bet. It is a moment of excitement. You can feel it in the air. People stop to see what will happen. Until that moment of "all in," the player is not completely invested. He's holding back for other opportunities. Like a gambler risking it all, your "all in" moment is when you show your real conviction and commitment to exceptionalizing it. Your strategy is clear, and your adrenaline is high as you commit to the "all in" bet.

It's time to fully commit to exceptional performance. You need to stop holding back. Half-heartedly trying won't cut it in today's business world. You have to fully invest your resources, time, and effort. You need to create your strategy to *Exceptionalize It!* That strategy must reflect a total commitment to elevating your performance to an exceptional level. You need to go "all in."

EXCEPTIONALIZE IT!™

Examine your commitment to *Exceptionalize It!* every day. Are you all in?

THE Ultimate Question

Now the journey starts.
In everything you do
there is one question
you ought to ask.

―――――――――――

Did I *Exceptionalize It!?*

―――――――――――

WITH GRATITUDE

For me, exceptionalism starts with expressing gratitude for all the good in your life. A book, like many other creations, is not a solo sport. It is a team sport. Even though some of the players are not aware of their participation, they nevertheless make a significant contribution to its success. These players are the people whose ideas I've read or heard and learned something from, people who I've had the privilege to work with, and people who have helped me in some way. Their actions have impacted and shaped my thoughts and ideas.
To all of you, thank you. Keep inspiring the world.

To my editor Ginger Conlon, thank you for the support, insights and ideas that made the book what it is today.

To my team at Strativity—Rachel, Michael B., Michael S., Marsha, Marc, Ed, David, Lacey, Uriel, Joe and all our partners around the world—thank you for your support. To Karen Harris and the team at CMI Speakers, my appreciation for your efforts supporting my agenda and spreading the word.

To my children Dalya, Cheli, Liad, Netanel, and Ronya, thank you for tolerating my absence and loving me no matter what. To my life partner, Drora, I know you never signed up for me becoming a "miles millionaire"; thank you for supporting me in pursuing my passion.

Strativity Group:
Inspiring Exceptional Performance

When organizations are looking to exceptionalize their performance and achieve exceptional results, we are here to help. With a proven methodology and track record of success, Strativity Group delivers tools and programs to accelerate transformation. We measure our success by a single word: execution.

For over 140 of the most exciting brands in the world, we have delivered transformation programs that touched 200 million customers and 300,000 employees in 21 countries.

Our services include:

- Diagnostics Tools

- Consulting Services

- Culture Transformation Programs

- Innovation Workshops

- Leadership Programs

- Learning Experiences

Committed to exceptionalizing it?
Let us bring our passion, tools, and methodology to your organization to achieve new performance heights.

For more information and inspiration visit: www.strativity.com

To contact us: info@strativity.com

Connect on Twitter: @LiorStrativity

For speaking engagements contact:
Karen Harris at CMI, karen@cmispeakers.com

CPSIA information can be obtained
at www.ICGtesting.com
Printed in the USA
FFOW05n1123220414